5 HABITS OF SUCCESSFUL PEOPLE

A VERY EFFECTIVE WAY TO ENSURE ULTIMATE SUCCESS IN ALL WORKS OF LIFE.

ANDREW L. HILTON

All rights reserved. No part of this publication may be reproduced, distributed, or
transmitted in any form or by any means, including photocopying, recording, or other electronic or mechanical methods, without the prior written permission of the publisher, except in the case of brief quotations embodied in reviews and certain other non-commercial uses permitted by copyright law.
Copyright © 2022. Andrew L. Hilton

Chapter 1 Waking up Early

Can we analyse things objectively for a moment? For the vast majority, it's challenging to get up first thing, particularly when it's as yet dim. However, many fruitful individuals say, "On the off chance that you win the morning, you win the day."
 There is a wide range of prosaisms about rising right on time. There's the one about the timely riser getting the worm, to which I generally answer that I don't need the worm.
 There are countless advantages to getting up right on time, from better execution in school to be more ready to adhere to an eating routine.

What are the Advantages of Getting up Ahead of schedule

Actual Assists You with Supporting a Better Eating regimen. Individuals who get up mid will generally have breakfast. At the same time, later risers are many times surging out the entryway and need to get something helpful (for example, unfortunate), or they skirt the dinner through and through.

The issue with skipping breakfast is that it prompts more unfortunate dietary patterns later in the day. If you're ravenous because you missed a feast, the donut in the lunchroom might be too enticing to even think about standing up to.

Assists Your Skin With looking Sound

Following an evening of relaxing rest, our skin is at its best first thing. Also, if you're a go-getter, you can exploit the morning hours to give your skin some additional attention.

Like the morning meal model above, individuals who rise and shine later in the day will often zero in less on solid morning propensities like hydrating and working out, which oxygenates your blood and advance sound skin. Early morning risers can likewise utilise the additional chance to shed, saturate and scrub.

Individuals who get up early likewise will have customary dozing propensities (dissimilar to the evening people who keep whimsical resting plans). An anticipated rest routine guarantees that your skin gets a legitimate chance to revive.

It gives You Additional Opportunities to Exercise.

I partake in an after-work exercise centre meeting however much the following individual. Yet, I'll confess to missing a fair number of exercises due to responsibilities at the workplace or with my loved ones. What's more, sometimes, I'm drained following an entire day of work!

You're more opposed to having a reason when you practice in the first part of the day. Also, you'll find that your morning exercise will keep you empowered the entire day.

Mental Better Focus

Beginning your day very early works on your fixation. As well as having the option to zero in on objectives and undertaking records without being interfered with by relatives or colleagues, starting early intends that when you get to work or school, you've had hours to adjust yourself to the day appropriately. You'll be more ready during top hours, therefore. Improves your Efficiency Best individuals report up at 5 am or considerably prior. Go-getters will generally be more beneficial for various reasons, including Having the additional opportunity to zero in on significant errands while the remainder of the world is sleeping.

This additionally means fewer interferences. Minds will generally be most ready in the first part of the day. On the off chance that you're ready to concentrate without interferences promptly in the day, you'll accomplish more. You will often pursue better choices and think more plainly toward the beginning of the day than in the early evening and night. Putting forth your objectives first thing will assist you with accomplishing them. If you can figure out how to get ahead of schedule, you'll find that you have more energy over the day. It appears to be irrational, yet there are innumerable tributes. Profound Works on your Nature of Rest Keeping your body on a rest routine will make it simpler to nod off and awaken simultaneously every evening. This is significant for your body's interior clock. Assuming you head to sleep late and get up late at the end of the week, for instance, it's harder for your body to change. Individuals who rise and shine early are normally sleepier when it's the "ordinary" time to hit the hay. Moreover, being on an anticipated routine will assist you with dozing better every evening and waking up refreshed and revived.

Assists you With getting a charge out of Calm Time

Now and again, it astonishes me that not every person rises and shines prior. It's a wonder how it calms the world first thing. In addition to the fact that there are zero interruptions, which will permit you to appreciate harmony and calm, however, you'll likewise observe that your everyday drive is more straightforward, assuming you leave an hour sooner and beat all the traffic. Furthermore, you get to keep away from all that irritating office chatter about ends of the week and children and all the stuff you need to claim to think often about to be "considerate."

Tips On the most proficient method to Start Ahead of schedule

Begin Gradually Assuming you regularly get up at 8 am and conclude that tomorrow you need to be up by 5 am, you're getting yourself in a position for disappointment. Have a go at awakening only 15 minutes sooner every day. In about seven days, you'll have moved gradually up to the right around two hours!

Rest Ambitious. Begin hitting the hay sooner than you ordinarily would. That way, you'll get an adequate number of long rest periods and won't feel denied when the alert goes off. If you're not worn out when now is the right time to get a few zzzs, read a couple of pages of a book, particularly an exhausting one, and you'll be in la la land in the blink of an eye.

Set a Morning timer. Except if you normally awaken at your objective time each day, you will have to set a caution. I suggest putting it across the room, so you must get up to switch it off. I likewise set the caution to play an uplifting or lively tune to assist with poking me up. Something with a positive message or an energetic sound is greatly improved to awaken to than a progression of upsetting signals.

Get Out of the Room We've all switched off our alert and crept right once again into bed. It's so warm and comfortable, correct? Leave your room. Whether it's an outing to the restroom or the espresso producer, whenever you've put sufficient distance between yourself and that ecstatic astonishing sleeping pad, you'll observe that you're sufficiently conscious to begin the day.

Have a Valid justification. Your considerable rundown of crises isn't the driver that ought to spring you up each day. Consider something positive that you anticipate achieving. Perhaps you can see yourself as something like you'll get to go home early, assuming you get to work prior. Or on the other hand, on the off chance that you appreciate pondering but don't frequently have the opportunity, utilise that as motivation to get up and begin your day. Consider It as a Prize By rising early, you're compensating yourself. Attempt to recall that. If that is a sufficient inspiration, pay off yourself with a treat from your #1 café or an extra lengthy shower, assuming you figure out how to get up on time and without squeezing rest.

Utilise the Additional Time

Is there a book you've needed to peruse or a web-based class you've been considering signing up for? Utilise the additional time you get in the first part of the day to accomplish something that helps you develop and move along.

Eat Less Before Sleep time.

Even though eating before bed can make you tired, it's likewise been known to upset your rest and even reason bad dreams. If your stomach is protesting, attempt a relieving cup of natural tea for rest rather than a carb-filled nibble.

Pursue a Firm Choice to Get Up. Regardless of whether you let yourself know the night before that, you anticipate ascending before sunrise, practically like you have a subsequent character who assumes control over when the caution goes off and encourages you to return to rest. It's alarming. You must be firm to keep away from that disgusting beast in your mind. On the off chance that you can't dissuade it, then, at that point, you'll have to set up outer prompts in your current circumstance. I suggest updating my telephone about my responsibility or resting in my activity garments, so I'm prepared to begin my day when I awaken.

Chapter 2 Workouts

HERE'S The reason Effective Business people Work-out Consistently.
Bill Gates, Richard Branson, Mark Zuckerberg, and Tim Cook.
Might you think about what they all share, practically speaking?
You're right, assuming you speculated that they generally sent off extravagant organisations.
However, practically speaking, we need to discuss something different that they all share.
They all swear that customary activity is a fundamental piece of their prosperity.
In a new blog entry, Branson said: "I truly question that I would have been as fruitful in my vocation (and cheerful in my own life) in the event that I hadn't generally put significance on my well-being and wellness."
Science backs this thought as well. Concentrates on demonstrating how ordinary activity can work on your emotional wellness, memory, and your energy levels and encourage you in general.
They're all appealing recommendations and aren't simply restricted to Chief's - everyone can receive the rewards of the standard activity.
So we should accept an inside and out take a gander at how customary activity can help business visionaries across the globe, how you can begin constructing an ordinary workout daily schedule for yourself, and which practices other effective business people depend on.
Practice Builds Your Energy Levels

Trust us - exercise can be far superior for expanding your energy levels than that huge mug of espresso you have each day.

Stand by; how might that be valid?

With each exercise, your body discharges endorphins, serotonin, and dopamine.

They could sound extravagant; however, they're generally known as "bliss chemicals."

Assuming that you've at any point finished an extraordinary exercise and felt awesome, even though you're depleted, you know direct what those bliss chemicals feel like while they're hurrying through your body.

Furthermore, it isn't simply satisfaction you'll feel after you've been working out - you'll likewise feel stimulated and prepared to get done with additional jobs in your day.

It could sound amazing; however, practice builds your blood dissemination and fortifies your heart muscle. It makes it simpler for your body to make energy - a mutually beneficial arrangement.

Thus, if you consistently commit a break of your week to exercises, your body will figure out how to normally deliver more endorphins quicker, which will pass on you with more energy to accomplish more in your day.

Workout Practising Builds Your Imagination and Focus

It turns out that those satisfaction chemicals aren't only perfect for expanding your energy levels - they're also perfect for pumping your innovative energies.

Whenever you've completed your exercise, you'll be prepared to handle undertakings that require inventiveness and have the energy to follow them the entire way.

However, it isn't soon after an exercise that you'll see a spike in imagination - you'll probably see that you're more focused during your exercises.

One little stunt which I've tracked down assists with exploiting the elevated center that I feel during an exercise is to welcome a scratch pad with me during my exercises.

This helps me in two ways:

I can follow my arranged activities and scribble down any significant subtleties about how my body feels every day.

I have a spot to record any groundbreaking thoughts I think of or jot down any new systems I concoct that could be useful to me to conquer the day ahead.

A journal isn't necessary - I could simply take my telephone to the gym equipment.

That is, on the off chance I didn't get occupied with such ease.

Truly, I've tracked down that carrying my telephone with me to tinker with during the breaks between my activities is such an efficient executioner.

Assuming I take my telephone with me, I find that my exercises take more time, are less extreme, and I'm even less inclined to finish all that I need to accomplish. No part of that is great.

In any case, you'll encounter an elevated center when you exercise - ensure you exploit it.

Practice Is Perfect for Emotional wellness.

A business venture can be unpleasant, as can any calling.

Actually: there will constantly be a couple of high-need errands you'll have to deal with on some random day.

It very well may be not difficult to zero in on the endless progression of work that you'll have to finish.

What's more, we've proactively spoken about ordinary activity and the advantages that it can bring to your actual well-being.

Yet, standard activity can likewise do some amazing things for your emotional wellness, particularly regarding managing pressure.

You'll have a mind-boggling feeling of prosperity after you have your pulse up.

You'll have the option to involve practice as a separation strategy, and you'll have the option to withdraw yourself from your day-to-day stresses and spotlight on something else entirely for a brief period. Something that you can feel is pursuing bettering yourself.

Furthermore, you'll have the option to take the energy you'd typically spend stressing over the amount of work you possess or how well you want to perform and center it into working on your well-being for the future - intellectually and truly.

You can take the energy you'd ordinarily spend stressing about the work you want to finish and centre it on working on your well-being - intellectually and truly.

Practising Toward the beginning of the day

Starting ahead of schedule to ensure I get my exercise dispenses with perhaps of the most concerning issue that I looked before - feeling excessively drained by the day's end to try and go to the recreational centre.

I know, I know. It's difficult to get up ahead of schedule.

Getting up considerably before getting an exercise in? Unimaginable,

To that end, I needed to examine it first in this book, we are talking about propensities, and beneficial routines are difficult to dominate; however, it gets more straightforward with time, and you will appreciate it.

I used to be a sequential finish-of-day exerciser, yet I've never contemplated thinking back since I changed to morning exercises.

There are a couple of motivations behind why I've cherished the switch, and negative, it's not because I appreciate tormenting myself.

Above all else, I find that morning exercises truly set an extraordinary vibe for the afternoon.

I once saw a discourse from Naval commander William McRaven, who talked about how making your bed is the main errand of your day.

Without a doubt, making your bed each day could appear paltry, yet it truly adds consistency to your everyday practice and permits you to achieve something just after you awaken.

I see morning exercises precisely the same way, aside from being considerably more successful. Try to keep your hat on; an hour of exercise will provide you with a lot more noteworthy sensation of achievement than making your bed will.

You'll likewise have to think that night exercises, particularly those that fall later than 8 pm, could disturb your rest.

Furthermore, in particular, morning exercises will often be a lot simpler to adhere to.

In the event that you're in any way similar to me, by far, most of your social responsibilities and get-togethers will happen at night.

That implies you'll have to pick between a gathering with the draw-up bar or your companions at your #1 plunge bar.

Try not to place yourself in that situation - simply finish in the first part of the day.

Building a Workout Daily Schedule

Integrating standard activity into your routine can help you both genuinely and intellectually.

In any case, if you've never truly been into exercise or battled to adhere to an everyday practice previously, it tends to be hard to imagine yourself exploiting those advantages in the long haul.

The research found that it just requires 66 days to coordinate a well-being and wellness routine in your life.

By all accounts, 66 days could appear to be quite a while; however, we should separate that figure.

Sixty-six days is 18% of your year.

Thus, if you start a pristine well-being and wellness routine toward the beginning of January and stick at it, you'll have coordinated it into your life toward the beginning of Spring.

Envision how the remainder of your year would go if you've previously had such a beneficial outcome from the get-go.

At the point when you take a gander at it according to that viewpoint, 66 days truly seems don't seem like anything.

Be that as it may, likewise with most things throughout everyday life, an ideal way to place yourself in a good position is to design ahead of time.

You should investigate how you can fabricate a workout routine that works for you.

Put forth Your Objectives.

Your initial step to building a workout schedule you can adhere to will be to concoct an objective you need to accomplish.

Perhaps it's dropping a couple of pounds, acquiring some muscle, or getting fitter for a game.

Anything it is - ensures you write it down and stick to it.

Your objective will be your north star - it'll be what you go to while looking for inspiration.

Pick Your Exercise Times

A significant piece of making a workout schedule that you can follow reliably is saving the hours of the day when you need to go to the rec center.

Find holes in your timetable that you can commit to working out, and make an honest effort to adhere to them.

Furthermore, make sure to pay attention to your body. If you're not feeling great or you're worn out, perhaps it's anything but smart to do your full exercise.

In any case, you must appear - a fragmented exercise is far superior to no exercise by any means.

Pick Activities Which Match Your Objectives

Whenever you've saved your desired objectives to accomplish and the times while you will pursue them, you'll have to figure out how you will accomplish them.

There are a lot of free assets accessible which can furnish you with exercise tips and deceives relying upon your objectives.

I like watching YouTube recordings while searching for new activities (since recordings assist me with understanding the mechanics of the activity better) or some inspiration.
Don't hesitate for even a moment to Have A great time.
The last thing you need while you're practicing is to feel exhausted.
That will drain your inspiration and hamper your advancement.
You can give working a shot with a companion, attend a wellness class, or join a games group.
There are a lot of choices accessible, so take a stab at dabbling with your daily schedule to find what truly works for you.

How Fruitful Business visionaries Exercise

We've previously covered the advantages of activity and pointed you to the correct bearing for when you need to make your own activity plan.
We should investigate the workout schedules of the absolute best business people on earth.
Tony Robbins
Grant-winning creator and business visionary Tony Robbins spends only 15 minutes each day on his exercises.
Be that as it may, what they need in length, they compensate for in power.
This is the thing he once said when he was acquainting his gym routine everyday practice with someone:
"You ought to feel like you're going to bite the dust, however you're not."
It's an extreme exercise, and it's not suggested for everyone, but rather Robbins swears that it's a vital piece of his prosperity.
Richard Branson
English business person Richard Branson, an organizer behind the Virgin Gathering, integrates his activity into his morning schedule.
Branson generally participates in practices that increment cardiovascular perseverance, similar to tennis and kitesurfing, and centers around "having some good times."
Furthermore, it's essential to note that he general attempts to follow up his exercise with a sound breakfast - which we accept is necessary to a useful morning schedule.
Mark Zuckerberg
Facebook's President is a major strength for any of the advantages of practice in a business venture.

He once said: "Doing anything well requires energy, and you simply have significantly more energy when you're fit."
He attempts to get in around three weekly exercises and generally picks running meetings with his dog.
Oprah Winfrey
Oprah Winfrey is another business person who depends on working out because she needs to "feel invigorated."
Her standard is that she attempts to accomplish something each day that assists her with feeling dynamic - this ordinarily converts into yoga meetings and attempts to hit the 10,000 stage count.
She's such an exercise fan, and she does interviews while on the treadmill:
Presently It's Your Move
Regarding working out, the key is to figure out what turns out best for your body and your timetable and shape a propensity around it.
Assuming you will construct your gym routine daily practice in the wake of perusing this post, ensure that you give your all to stick at it.
Keep in mind that 66 days is the enchanted number.
Furthermore, if you're battling with inspiration, recall your objectives, think about taking classes, working out with companions, or in any event, recruiting a fitness coach to help you along.
I'll leave you with this statement from effective business visionary Josh Steimle:
"If I somehow managed to quit practicing on the grounds that I felt that being a decent entrepreneur was a higher need, then, at that point, unexpectedly I would wind up a more regrettable entrepreneur than I was the point at which it was a lower need."
Thus, presently it's over to you.

Chapter 3 Life Long Learning

The key to long-lasting achievement is deep-rooted learning.
The most active, best individuals on the planet track down basically an hour to learn regularly.
Michael Simmons
Supporter, Forbes, Fortune, HBR, and Time
"In my entire life, I have known no wise individuals (over a wide topic region) who didn't peruse constantly — none. Zero." — Charlie

Munger, Independent tycoon, and Warren Buffett's long-lasting colleague

For what reason did the most active individual on the planet, previous president Barack Obama, read an hour daily while in office?

Why has the best financial backer, Warren Buffett, focused intently on perusing and thinking all through his vocation?

Why has the world's most extravagant individual, Bill Entryways, read a book seven days during his vacation? Moreover, why has he required a yearly fourteen-day perusing excursion throughout his whole vocation?

For what reason do the world's savviest and most active individuals find one hour daily for conscious learning (the 5-hour rule)? In contrast, others rationalise how occupied they are. What do they see that others don't?

The response is straightforward: Learning is the absolute best speculation we can make in recent memory. Or on the other hand, as Benjamin Franklin said, "An interest in information pays the well-being."

This understanding is essential to prevailing in our insight economy, yet a couple of individuals acknowledge it. Fortunately, getting a more significant amount of information is necessary when you comprehend the worth of data. Devote yourself to consistent learning.

Information is the new cash.

"Scholarly capital will continuously best monetary capital." — Paul Tudor Jones, independent, wealthy person, business visionary, financial backer, and humanitarian.

We spend our lives gathering, aching for, and agonising over cash. When we say we "lack the opportunity" to discover some new information, it's typical because we are hotly committing our opportunity to bring in cash. However, something is going on right well that is changing the connection between money and information.

We are toward the start of a time of what prestigious futurist Peter Diamandis calls quick demonetization, in which innovation is delivering beforehand costly items or administrations a lot less expensive — or even free.

This graph from Diamandis' book Overflow shows how we've demonetized $900,000 worth of items and administrations you could have bought between 1969 and 1989.

This demonetization will advance from now on. Mechanised vehicle armadas will dispense with perhaps our most incredible buy: A vehicle. Computer-generated reality will make costly encounters, for example, showing up at a show or playing golf, quickly accessible at a much lower cost. While the contrast between the real world and computer-generated reality is practically unique right now, the pace of progress in VR is outstanding.

While schooling and medical care costs have risen, advancement in these fields will probably prompt possible demonetization. Numerous higher instructive foundations, for instance, have inheritance expenses to help various layers of order and to upkeep their grounds. More current foundations are tracking down approaches to decisively bring down costs by offering their administrations solely web-based, zeroing in just on preparing for popular, lucrative abilities, or having bosses who select understudies sponsor the expense of educational cost.

At last, new gadgets and advancements, for example, CRISPR, the XPrize Tricorder, better diagnostics through manufactured consciousness, and decreased cost of genomic sequencing, will upset the medical services framework. These advancements and different ones like them will be below the average expense of medical care by zeroing in on counteraction instead of fix and the board.

While labour and products are becoming demonetized, information is becoming progressively significant.

Maybe the best illustration of the rising worth of specific types of information is oneself driving vehicle industry. Sebastian Thrun, a pioneer behind Google X and Google's self-driving vehicle group, gives the case of Uber paying $700 million for Otto, a six-month-old organisation with 70 workers, and of GM burning through $1 billion on their securing of Journey. He presumes that in this industry, "The going rate for ability these days is $10 million."

That is $10 million for each talented labourer, and keeping in mind that that is the most staggering model, it's not only valid for unimaginably uncommon and rewarding specialised abilities. Individuals who distinguish abilities required for future positions — e.g., information examiner, item architect, actual advisor — and immediately learn them are ready to win.

The people who buckle down through their vocation yet don't take time from their timetable to learn continually will be the new "in danger" bunch. They risk staying stuck on the base bar of the worldwide contest and risk losing their responsibilities to robotization, similarly as somewhere in the range of 2000 and 2010 when robots supplanted 85% of blue-collar positions.

Why?

Individuals at the lower part of the financial stepping stool are being pressed more and remunerated less. At the same time, those at the top have more open doors and are paid more than any other time in recent memory. The dichotomy is that the issue isn't an absence of occupations. Instead, it lacks individuals with the right abilities and informations to fill the position.

An Atlantic article catches the mystery: "Bosses across ventures and locales have griped for quite a long time about an absence of talented specialists, and their objections are borne out in US business information. In July [2015], the quantity of occupation postings arrived at its most significant level ever, at 5.8 million, and the joblessness rate was easily beneath the post-The Second Great War normal. However, simultaneously, north of 17 million Americans are either jobless, not working yet keen on tracking down work, or accomplishing seasonal work yet seeking to everyday work."

So, we can perceive how information is progressively turning into its own significant and remarkable type of cash at a top level. All in all, information is the new cash. Like cash, information frequently fills in as a mode of trade and store of significant worth.

Be that as it may, in contrast to cash, when you use information or part with it, you don't lose it. Moving information anyplace on the planet is free and moment. It's worth mixtures over the long run quicker than cash. It tends to be changed into numerous things money can't purchase, like genuine connections and elevated degrees of emotional prosperity. It assists you with achieving your objectives quicker and better. It's amusing to secure. It makes your cerebrum work better. It grows your jargon, making you a superior communicator. It assists you with imagining greater possibilities and past your conditions. It places your everyday routine in context by helping you encounter many carries on within one life through others' encounters and shrewdness.

Previous president Obama impeccably makes sense of why he was so dedicated to perusing during his administration in a New York Times interview (paywall): "when occasions move so rapidly thus much data is sent," he said, perusing empowered him to sporadically "dial back and get point of view" and "the capacity to get from another person's perspective." These two things, he added, "have been priceless to me. Whether they've made me a superior president I can't say. In any case, what I can say is that they have permitted me to kind of keep up with my equilibrium throughout eight years, since this is a spot that comes at you firm and doesn't ease up.'"

Six fundamentals abilities to dominate the new information economy

"The unskilled of the 21st century won't be the individuals who can't peruse and compose; however, the people who can't learn, forget, and relearn." — Alvin Toffler.

How would we become familiar with the correct information and have it pay off? The six focuses beneath act as a structure to assist you with starting to respond to this inquiry. I also made a top-to-bottom online class on Figuring out How To Discover that you can look at free of charge.

1. Recognize important information with impeccable timing. The worth of data isn't static. It changes as an element of how many others consider it and how uncommon it is. As new innovations mature and reshape enterprises, there is often a shortage of individuals with the required abilities, which creates the potential for high remuneration. Given the great pay, more individuals are immediately prepared, and the typical payment diminishes.

2. Learn and dominate that information rapidly. Opportunity windows are brief. People should exploit them when they see them. This implies having the option to master new abilities quickly. In the wake of perusing many books, I've viewed that understanding and utilising mental models is quite possibly the most widespread ability everybody ought to acquire. It gives areas of strength for information that applies across each field. So when you hop into another field, you have previous information you can use to learn more quickly.

3. Impart the worth of your abilities to other people. Individuals with similar skills can order various pay rates and expenses in light of how well they're ready to impart and convince others. This capacity persuades others that the capabilities you have are significant is a "multiplier expertise." Many individuals go through years dominating essential specialised expertise and practically no time defeating this multiplier expertise.

4. Convert information into cash and results. There are numerous ways of changing data into esteem in your life. A couple of models incorporate getting and getting a line of work that compensates fairly, receiving a pay increase, fabricating a fruitful business, selling

your insight as an expert, and building your standing by turning into an idea chief.

5. Figure out how to put resources into figuring out how to get the best yield monetarily. Every one of us needs to see the right "portfolio" of books, online courses, and authentication/degree projects to assist us with accomplishing our objectives with

Chapter 4 Goal Oriented

How To Be Goal-Oriented?
Having goals is, in every case, great. Turning out to be more objective and arranged may assist you with accomplishing the achievements you need more quickly. From work objectives to life and family objectives, there could be many justifications for why you'd need to accomplish specific things. This section will investigate being objectively situated, as well as tips to turn out to be all the more so. You can achieve anything you need to, giving you find the correct ways to accomplish your objectives.

What Does Being Objective Arranged Mean?

Objective situated implies you endeavour to get done with explicit responsibilities to arrive at a specific result. It means that you are driven and roused by a feeling of direction: either throughout everyday life, work, or something different that has your consideration and responsibility. Here are a few abilities and characteristics that help people who are objective situated succeed:
Arranging and association
Energy
Mindfulness
Using time productively
Logical
How Would You Turn out to be More Objective Situated?
There are numerous manners by which you can turn out to be more objective arranged. There are specific techniques you can give a shot to be a more coordinated and propelled person, which will help your time-usage abilities like this. This implies that you can accomplish your objectives speedier.

For what reason is it vital to be objective and arranged? Assuming that you make objectives without asking yourself what your natural assets and values are first, you could put yourself on the road to success and disillusionment. Then again, on the off chance that you set no expectations by any stretch of the imagination, you could bob through life like a pinball doing what others need without achieving what means a lot to you.

Dread not.

The following are;

Eight viital ways of being objective situated utilising the Imagine strategy (Final stage - Settling - Worth - Motivation - Superpowers - Lingerie - Receptiveness - Sustenance) that will assist you with making a fruitful, significant life:

1. Begin Given the End

To guarantee that you make objectives that matter, stand back and inspect your life according to a more extensive viewpoint. Contemplate the cheerful completion you might want to accomplish, the "E" in Imagine, and work in reverse to decide how you'll arrive.

For instance, assuming you want to create objectives for yourself throughout the following five years, record where you might want to be expertly and a long time from now.

Where do you see yourself according to work? How's your everyday life? What sort of companions and social care group do you have? What are your side interests?

Then, ask yourself where you might want to be one year from now compared to what you want to achieve in five years. Work the response out in sufficient detail, so it appears genuine to you. Then, at that point, ask yourself where you might want to be three months from now. Be explicit.

And one month or multi-week? What one little activity might you at some point require this week to draw nearer to accomplishing your groundbreaking strategy?

This exercise is a tomfoolery and educational method for fixing your objectives with the master plan of your life so you won't squander your valuable energy on fleeting interests and others' projects.

2. Make Settled Objectives

The most productive method for accomplishing your objectives is to settle things to do inside them, the first "N" in Imagine. Objective-situated individuals become explicit about when, where, and how they'll arrive at their targets by separating them into sub-objectives.

Make your desires testing yet not excessively hard. Everyone ought to be quantifiable. Rather than expressing "I might want to compose a book," take a stab at setting an aim, for example, "I might want to compose two hours per day, four times each week," and imprint space on your schedule for it.

Make your points positive and monitor your advancement. Rather than business objectives like "I might want to stop my smelling position," ponder what a helpful profession would resemble. Attempt "I might want to create instructive toys with similar individuals in a virtual office," and afterwards convey your list of qualifications to organisations with matching employment opportunities.

Concoct elective pathways to your objectives so that if one doesn't work, you'll have plan B set up. It's generally expected to fall flat and experience difficulties. This objective-arranged technique will assist you with pushing ahead on the pathway to your fantasies regardless.

3. Get Clear on Your Qualities

Before defining objectives, you must ask yourself what you genuinely esteem, the "V" in Imagine.

The central lament of individuals on their deathbeds is that they didn't experience their fantasies. Try not to let that be you. To try not to carry on with a daily existence brimming with "shoulds" and commitments, make a list of things to get. Write down what you truly need, and put every one of the reasons you figure you can't have it to the side.

Excessively Wrecked to Accomplish What You Want to Do?

Get the push you want to push ahead by snatching your FREE activity intended to end overpower, recover inspiration and get everything in order!

These desires can go from the material (like another vehicle) to the mental (high self-esteem), to the profound (internal harmony), to essentially anything you can imagine. What sort of life could be what you wanted to hear? It doesn't make any difference whether it appears unreachable or even insane.

Allowing yourself to wander off in a fantasy land about a rich and satisfying life is the initial step to getting it. Be sure your objectives address your spirit.

4. Set aside a few minutes for motivation

As you set your objectives, contemplate how you can track down free time to become objective-driven and get motivation in your life, the first "I" in Imagine.

Americans set forth the most extended effort hours and get the most limited paid time off worldwide. Any of us "fortunate" enough to have occupations have added one more day to our week of work since we presently browse work messages and calls from home. It's not difficult to see why it's challenging to remain persuaded toward explicit objectives in the long haul.

The second lament of the withering is that they wished they didn't buckle down. Research shows that individuals who participate in imaginative leisure activities and side undertakings are more joyful and thrive more in life since they can produce groundbreaking thoughts and put themselves out there uniquely. Feeling empowered and perky, they accomplish more significantly quicker, become better issue solvers, and get better assessments at work.

5. Structure Objectives Around Your Superpowers

Research shows that individuals are bound to succeed when they foster their regular assets, the "S" in Imagine, and then work on their shortcomings.

Every one of us has an outstanding reason throughout everyday life. The vast majority of us don't understand it, however, because we've been compelled to adjust to another person's concept of who we ought to be. Feeling of dread toward change and remaining in our usual ranges of familiarity hinder our development. Stretch yourself and face a challenge if you have any desire to figure out what compels your heart to sing.

Make an activity arrangement to make a daily existence in which you express your superpowers consistently, whether through your job, a significant side task, a noble motivation, careful nurturing, humanitarian effort, or whatever else flashes your advantage. This objective arranged procedure ensures you'll flourish at work and home.

6. Set aside a few minutes for underwear

While defining your objectives, make sure to cut time for your underwear, the second "I" in Imagine. Underwear alludes to dear companions or individuals you have cosy associations with.

The fourth lament of the perishing is that they were excessively occupied with seeing their companions. Make it a highlight to associate with genuine companions, individuals you can go to for compassion when you want it, trust in about most things, and be your actual self around.

Another Cigna study shows that almost 50% of Americans feel alone or left out. As Dr Julianne Holt-Lunstad at Brigham Youthful

College, the unfavourable impacts of depression are equivalent to smoking 15 cigarettes daily. That's what she cautions:

"Dejection and social disengagement are connected to around a 30 percent expanded hazard of suffering a heart attack or creating coronary corridor disease." [6]

Being with your companions isn't just great for your spirit. However, it is additionally fundamental for your well-being and prosperity. Could you put it in your objectives?

7. Open up Genuinely

While making your objective arranged life, incorporate ways you can get serious about your sentiments, the "O" in Imagine. The third lament of the perishing is that they wish they'd dared to communicate their actual sentiments instead of stuffing their feelings down to keep harmony with others.

To lead a satisfying life, focusing on talking and acting genuinely with others is essential instead of concealing your actual sentiments. As per Dr Leslie Becker-Phelps

"Begin with recognizing your feelings (for example furious, hurt) and understanding what set off you to feel as such."

She prescribes you attempt to comprehend your sentiments and practice self-empathy for having them. At the point when you're more settled, attempt to comprehend the individual who upsets you. This will help you regard and care about yourself and the other individual.

If there is somebody you want to converse with or a circumstance you might want to determine, honour your sentiments. Whether it be composing a letter, settling on a telephone decision, or visiting somebody you haven't found in years, put it on your objective rundown.

Make sure to meet in a protected climate if you're defying somebody who has manhandled or hurt you. Come clean from your perspective, and attempt to be thoughtful.

Sharing your real sentiments might unite you, and it may not. It doesn't exactly make any difference how the other individual answers. What makes a difference is that you communicate your actual self. Practice profound genuineness all the time by adding it to your objectives.

8. Sustain Bliss

To be more objective, arranged and prevail throughout everyday life, sustain individuals and exercises that give you pleasure, the last "N" in Imagine.

The fifth lament of individuals on their deathbed is that they wished they'd allow themselves to be more joyful. All things being equal, they remained caught in old examples and claimed to be content when they weren't.

If you could do without your work, make it an objective to search for another place that adjusts your check to your motivation. If you are innovatively disapproved, ponder transforming your purposeful venture into a business you love. If you have different interests, consider chasing after a slice profession (e.g., publicist/coder/vocation mentor).

According to Forbes Magazine, many organizations are starting to see the worth in recruiting part-time workers that vary from their principal employments. You'll acquire various floods of pay and experience important satisfaction in your life.

If you are discontent with your marriage or heartfelt connection, put forth an objective to take care of business. Do you have to go to advising? Do you have to continue?

If you're wavering about keeping a companion in your life, be objective and situated about accepting reality on the issue. Deal with yourself by finishing positive everyday responsibilities, such as taking yoga classes or getting an essential back rub.

Anything you do, make it an objective to show empathy as frequently as possible on the grounds that it will support your happiness.[10] By helping other people out of luck, you not exclusively can diminish their misery. Yet, you can likewise make yourself more joyful than you could by straightforwardly chasing after exercises to fulfil you.

Last Contemplations

In outline, the Imagine strategy tells you the best way to mix examples from the five-second thoughts of the perishing with successful objective setting procedures that middle around your assets to become objective driven.

It might appear to be a great deal of work from the outset, however, in truth, it ought to take you about an hour to sort out a rundown of objectives while keeping these rules. Why not exchange an hour of sitting in front of the TV or participating in online entertainment to do this, all things equal? You can constantly get on the web and sit in front of the television later to reimburse yourself for becoming more objective arranged.

You should risk all that to acquire by investigating what might compel your heart to sing. It merits putting resources into yourself along these lines. You can make a day-to-day existence that thoroughly shakes by setting the goal.

As the thirteenth-century Persian writer, Rumi composed,
"What you seek is seeking you."

Chapter 5 Streams Of Income

Why You Need Multiple Streams of Income Starting Right Now
However, many individuals may not understand that they have different lucrative regions. Also, others may not consider why various cash surges truly matter.

Not make any difference what range you fall under; you
staggered on this post for a reason. Ideally, you'll leave away with a superior comprehension of why various floods of pay can be so significant.

What Are Different Surges of Pay?

The idea is straightforward, and you likely needn't bother with an authoritative definition to genuinely understand what it implies. However, we should, in any case, assemble something to get in total agreement.

Making numerous revenue streams permits a person to have different income sources that are coming in. This sets you in an ideal situation to be ready on the off chance that one type of revenue fizzles. Presently you have something to back up on.

What's cool about this ongoing computerized age is there are many ways of bringing in steady additional cash, whether detached or dynamic. In any case, before we get into specific models, I need to cover the advantages of having numerous surges of pay.

The Advantages of Numerous Surges of Pay
Like the definition, you presumably have a brilliant thought or can surmise why having more than one pay source is really smart. However, we should investigate these a touch more exhaustively.

Assists you with getting more cash
I mean, the most apparent benefit is producing more cash. This can assist you with arriving at your monetary objectives, carry on with a more peaceful life (as long as you have a way of life expansion

under wraps), and assist with taking care of any obligations you might have quicker.

Ponder every one of the open doors and opportunities having cash coming into you and your family from different streams can do.

Some monetary assurance of employment cutback

The more significant part of individuals are working for an organization and have 9-5 calls. Sadly sooner or later, you might be necessary for a layoff, which is in no way enjoyable. I was back in 2014, just before Christmas!

While I was a piece stunned, I had previously been accomplishing some temporary labour for an organization as an afterthought and promptly connected with increment my hours. I had a monetary pad of 20 hours every week to get some cash while I was on a hands-on chase.

Different streams will guarantee if an employment cutback occurs, you have some cash coming in your direction every month. It can ease some cash pressure that an employment cutback can bring.

Hit withdrawal from the workforce objectives

Many individuals want to resign early; they could be in their 30s, 40s, or 50s. You might, in any case, deal with a portion of your revenue sources, yet beginning them early can likewise be your pass to exiting the workforce.

Not every person will have a significant league salary or make north of six figures in their professions, which might give saving and contributing restrictions.

However, various pay surges can raise your saving and contributing rates, which can compound speedier for you.

Exiting the workforce is likewise not reliant upon having a different flood of pay as many have done it with their salaried work. Yet, extra cash-producing streams can unquestionably help.

Expansion

One of the main monetary terms to learn and live by is enhancement. A clear perspective isn't tying up your resources in one place. I know, buzzword explanation has been utilized to death, yet it's the most effective way to depict it.

Enhancing is a significant methodology for fruitful financial planning; you must spread your cash to various resources for security during slumps.

The model in the securities exchange requires a blend of stocks, bonds, and perhaps some land.

In any case, this idea applies to how you bring in cash as well; you need to have various ways of income-producing streams. You could acquire more on your everyday employment than others; however, you ought to have other streams to balance, assuming that something would occur.

It can make you a tycoon quicker.

This isn't to say you'll turn into a mogul short-term or that it is straightforward. You'll have to invest the effort; however, various streams are an integral approach to turning into a mogul and keeping up with that abundance throughout your lifetime.

Sorry if that was a misleading content title to you, yet it has truth to it. Having a couple of floods of pay with an intelligent individual budget and contributing propensities will have you hit mogul status quicker.

You may likewise have found out about the seven floods of pay, which is what the typical tycoon has. Also, a considerable number have more than that as well!

Yet, it appears to be legit, right? The more pay you have from various streams, the better your chances of turning into a tycoon and having high total assets.

Here are the seven various revenue streams with an exceptionally fundamental rundown:

Brought in - Cash acquired by taking care of business for another person.

Benefit: Cash is produced by selling something (labour and products).

Premium: This is cash accumulated by crediting money to the bank, government, another person, and so on.

Profits: Cash gets back to you (once in a while, month to month, quarterly, yearly) for possessing shares in an organization.

Capital Additions: Cash produced from expanded esteem in a resource you own.

Rental: When you lease a land resource like a house or business.

Eminence: Money you make from permitting items, thoughts, or cycles of yours.

Extra: Need to watch and keep up with your total assets simply? I suggest Individual Capital; it's allowed to join and utilize. They offer other free devices and an abundance of benefits as well.

Instances of Numerous Surges in Pay

With regard to constructing other surges of pay, you have various choices. The advanced age has set out other open doors to bring in cash at any additional time.

Be that as it may, rather than posting each model, underneath are only a portion of the incredible level normal ones you should consider.

Your Salaried Work: For a great many people, your 9-5 salaried work will be your essential type of revenue. It's where your predictable compensation comes in. Yet, your objective ought to be to make as much as possible and use any representative advantages. Are you searching for more? This is the way to build your compensation.

Optional compensation - I allude to this as your mate's pay, which can add another pleasant revenue source. Perhaps it's full-time pay or part-time, one way or another; this other compensation is an extraordinary method for guaranteeing your family has another revenue source.

Your Speculations: The other regular stream of pay you'll begin creating is through your interests in the securities exchange utilizing 401k, Roth IRA, and so forth. Your speculations regularly pay out as profits and capital additions. Moreover, you will not be contacting any of this cash until retirement (typically); however, it is producing pay for you. Here are a few essential inquiries to pose to yourself before putting resources into the securities exchange.

Online Business: The web has made it feasible for additional individuals to track down ways of having another revenue source. Numerous web-based organizations can drive part-time more than your full-time pay without much stretch. It tends to be anything from beginning a blog, selling things on eBay, selling your craft, outsourcing, Amazon FBA, and so on.

Gig Economy: The ascent of the gig economy has filled as of late on account of innovation organizations invigorating this new wave. Consider organizations like Uber, Airbnb, Lyft, and Wanderer, where you are paid for a particular undertaking through the stage. Can you get rich or do this full-time? Presumably not; however, it's another income stream to consider.

Rental Pay: Other than a portion of the expense benefits of claiming property and leasing, you can bring in some cash by simply leasing properties you could possess. To begin, you'll require an underlying cash flow, yet there is some incredible growing long-term financial stability potential. Land crowdfunding may be a decent other option for people who aren't prepared for this or don't have the underlying forthright money.

Last Considerations

Right now, you ought to see the worth of different floods of pay.

Do you have to have at least seven like a few tycoons do? Not actually; it depends on what and how you choose to create more pay.

The significant viewpoint is that you for sure ought to have multiple. Also, from the models above, you most likely have some if you are effective money management or have 401k/IRA.

In any case, if your monetary future siphons you up and you need more monetary security, search for 3-4 revenue sources. You can continuously grow as you settle in.

Recollect, numerous revenue streams can take time and work to fabricate. Yet, you will glean some helpful knowledge en route, guaranteeing you're on the correct way monetarily.

Conclusion

Success is Guaranteed

Let me repeat the most crucial communication of this entire book. It's this "Success is predictable."
You can be successful in numerous such areas in life
You have to make the mindset.
Success isn't a matter of luck, accident, or being in the right place at the right time. Success is as predictable as the sun rising in the east and setting in the west. By rehearsing the principles you have just learned, you'll move to the front of the line. You'll have an inconceivable advantage over people who don't know or don't exercise these ways and strategies. You'll have a gift that will give you the winning edge for the rest of your life and career.
Still, nothing in the world can stop, If you constantly and persistently do the effects that other successful people do.

www.ingramcontent.com/pod-product-compliance
Lightning Source LLC
Chambersburg PA
CBHW050328220526
45465CB00005B/2178